A Dolphin's Day

by Jeanne Baca Schulte
Illustrated by Brian Demeter

PEARSON

Glenview, Illinois • Boston, Massachusetts
Chandler, Arizona • Upper Saddle River, New Jersey

A baby dolphin is born.
A mother takes care of her baby.

Dolphins live together in a group.
The group is called a pod.
They work together as a team.

A dolphin gets stuck in a net.
Other dolphins help.
They push it up, up, up.

The dolphin gets out of the net.
Then it takes in air.

Now it is time to eat.
The dolphins herd fish together.
Then they take turns getting fish.

A shark is coming!
One dolphin makes a loud sound.
The sound warns others in the pod.

The dolphins swim away.
They are safe.